RICOCHET SCRIPT

RICOCHET SCRIPT

Poems by

Alexandra van de Kamp

Published by
Next Page Press
San Antonio, Texas
www.nextpage-press.com

ISBN: 978-1-7366721-1-2

Ricochet Script book team:
Laura Van Prooyen, Director and Editor
Joni Wallace, Assisting Editor
Sheila Black, Assisting Editor
Tina Posner, Consultant
Judy Jensen, Consultant
Sadie Clyne, Cover Image
Amber Morena, Book Design

For my mother, Patricia Woods

CONTENTS

RICOCHET SCRIPT

"My angels dance
on the tips of matches.
They have no wings."
   —KAREN VOLKMAN

"When all the details fit in perfectly,
something is probably wrong with the story."
   —CHARLES BAXTER

The Sound Engineer with His Castanets and Feathered Pillows

The wisteria is dusty today, sagging
with the tattered ends of summer. My vocabulary

hiccups: I say *Bermuda*
when I want to say *Cuba*. I say *anchovy*,

and my husband knows to translate:
black, Mediterranean olives. The birds settle

like exotic fruit in the trees (fruit
with gray wings and shiny

green bones, fruit that doesn't know
I am calling it *fruit*) and shadows flex

their spreading grimaces up
and down my arms and shoulders.

Each day advertises itself like a matinee,
although the bright wattage

of the title is often lost on me,
and the plot's key twist. Me, the member

of the audience who stumbles
into the theater, mid-action,

who finds out three days
after the fact, of the shooting,

of the boy turning to go,
but not fast enough,

of the cop and his jittery
gun (a gun that has no idea

we're calling it *gun*). Where's
the sound engineer

with his castanets, feathered pillows,
and soft mops to usher us

out of all of this? The trotting horses
and tiger's sensual purr close as breath

against my ear? Hand me a storyline
I can trust, give me five seconds of thunder,

blue and murderous, receding beyond
the pink umbrellas of a Long Island

August sunset, and I'll begin
to envision a supposed heaven, replete

with the flimsy armature
of the angels' wings, and their violins—

rain-warped, wisteria-thin.

If I Were the Writer of My Own Spy Thriller

There would be snow in at least seven scenes:
blue-edged snow scalloping
the Swiss chalet where the first murder

takes place. The murder
that will tilt my spy's trajectory
toward years of solitary, globetrotting ennui.

Would it be a lover who wrongfully
died? A colleague, who told bad jokes,
ate too many pistachio nuts, the brittle
shells cracking in his mouth?

So many potential
plots to a life, so many ricocheting
scripts, so many exotic,
jasmine-scented recipes for death. Where to edit

the undesirable furniture? Where to snip away
at the vague aromas
of a Connecticut summer?

I would ensure my protagonist's
passport had the fatigued look of an over-thumbed
bestseller. I would allow her to cross

borders as if they were soft and blank
as pond water. Spanish plum tomatoes,
in all their midday sweetness, would curtsy
their way through several scenes. There would be
at least one espresso sipped casually at 10 AM
somewhere in Italy, and in the evenings,

her nemesis would read Rimbaud
and Anne Sexton—his hitmen
having been instructed

and sent away. But he'd fail to drink in
the words the way he did his chilled Prosecco,
which would dribble
occasionally down his chin, unlike the misgivings
he'll never have.

And, please, no heads exploding in slow motion
like fleshy, enraged and gasping roses.

No death-defying showdowns (motorcycles
Cirque-du-Soleiling over rooftops and
market squares), unless they take place

in a city with well-funded art museums
and free admission for the public on Sundays.

And my spy? She'd pull muscles when scaling
walls, she'd slow down long enough
to spot the people next to her on the subway,

one of them sweating and reading Tolstoy.
She'd have second thoughts, and she'd bleed
when shot, the terrible, jarring bullet

interrogating her heart each time.

Dear Time,

I thought there was an agreement here,
a fistful of birds that I could carry

from one moment to the next
in my half-closed hands

without being bitten
by their peculiar beaks. A day,

I'm finding, is a letter written
in someone else's script, a kind of wobbly

transcription the air brushes along my lips.
The trees murmur like deceased

aunts spilling cups of tea in their
ginger laps. *Lips. Laps.* The lush insistence

of you, time, pushing against everything
we do. You are a shivering, unflinching

closeness, a tune we all have stuck in our heads,
as we lift blue towels from the washing machine,

drag our minds through the news,
tally the dead, frail as daffodils

trailing their stubborn pollen
along our outstretched arms.

I wake with a quaking inside me, a to-do list
of vitamin pills, the precise

wording of half-written emails, conversations
intricate as Medieval tapestries

glistening with their multitude of tiny threads.
I write to you, dear time, minister of fear

and sex and the hope of the body, to grab
at the visible tremor of a tree's

fog-laced leaves, to note the streetlamp
in a Magritte urban square—the oncoming

darkness momentarily stalled
before that quiet glow.

I want to stuff my mind
with all the living I can. Mortality be damned.

Let's relish another tablespoon
of that tarragon-seasoned lobster sauce

against the sheer glass
of a Houston skyline.

A delicate terror
builds within me.

Noon:

a pair of cellophane scissors
that snaps the day in two. How many

have wrapped like a breathless sash
about my waist, and how

many do I have left? Plump pouch
of time, midday grab bag

of petty thoughts
and grumpy disease, sugar packet

of dust crushed by the sun,
I want to look straight at you

and call your heady bluff. Each day
a cascading. Right now,

the afternoon sky emulsifies
into midnight, and pink peonies pop

the darkness like glow-in-the-dark toys
as rain gurgles gutters and plucks

brick walls. The variables tremble,
and another noon is gone in a confusion

of birdbaths and missed appointments.
I count (to keep account)

but such counting only divides
the loss into smaller,

more glittering proportions.

A Partial Cento with Middle Age Embedded into It

I lift my eyes and am chastened
by the angry heartbreak this world can bring.

So I settle into the rustling fabrics
of this October noon, its yellow-green

calico branches bobbing.
Odes to light fall short

every time. How to take in
what a day leaks out?

Kenneth White was killed after several teens
tossing rocks from atop an overpass

threw a large rock that struck him.
The object crashed

through the windshield of the vehicle
White was traveling in.

Odes on mortality
flounder every time.

The gray plastic chairs
in the backyard are casting

glossy shadows more precise
than they are. When does a prank

teeter into crime? When does
middle age sneak up on you,

cat burglar
with a velvet knife? I wish

I were a quicker study
of what unravels about me.

The British detective on TV
claims: "Life's just a series

of moments. That's all there is,"
as his elbow juts out

the car window. Dear reader,
is this too cinematographic

a register?
The dogs

howled/ someone recited
ominous verses to a child.

I drove back from the department
of public safety,

happy just to have survived it all.

Sunday Epistle

Dear Sunday, here we are again,
you and I, on that thinning cusp
between one week and the next. The sun
tilts its hat to the trees, and the breeze
has picked up, adding lutes and cymbals
to its translucent score. I forget
my happinesses all the time. I forget
how the leaves whisper their intermittent,
silvery names. I even forget
my husband's patience—
a space he carries inside
like a secret fruit waiting
to be peeled open. The sun
has shifted again. Each hour
a reshuffling of well-thumbed cards
in a game of light, luck,
and second chances I'll never be
an expert in. I've accrued a handful
of talents, but could I ever name
the one of most value? Perhaps,
my penchant for anything 70%
dark chocolate or my attention
to details: the floor-sweeping negligees
women wore in 1940s movies—
a whole genre of wardrobe
now lost to us. Or my knack for noting
the exact mustard-yellow
painted across my kitchen walls—
the simplest of facts sometimes
radiating: *This is your life.*

I opened up an unfinished autobiography
the other day by a writer I love. I found myself
in a library in her native West Indies,
where the librarian looks more ill
with each patron's book
she's stamping, and dies
a few days later. Oh, Sunday,
you are my weekly reckoning,
my trickle of light down
the sad wrist, my cooling cup
of tea, my indelible *what if*.

Writing Exercise with No Birds in It

I'm starved for some words today—
rounded and ridged morsels,

like the tender glazed donut
I placed into my mouth

a few hours ago, puffy fist
that slowly dissolved.

Each day lengthens its hyphenated
list of partial pleasures—red-charcoal wine

swiveled in a glass, ruby ocean
I shatter as I swallow.

Then, the abacus of anxiety
counts its oily, threadbare beads

inside me. I read
about angels in a dead poet's

poem (she died on a Sunday). Hers
is a sullen one,

who smokes *Luckys*. He
sticks around like a street-smart

kid with a crush, shadowing her
solitary life. Mine? She'd have

bruised wings, a hesitant creaking
of cartilage wafting about her.

When in the mood, she'd look up
unknown words in her dictionary

with its blue battered spine—
madrigal, cordgrass.

World news growls on
like a six-cylinder muscle car.

I read more, confuse *grenadiers*
with *grenadine,*

and toss pomegranate
grenades through light-flickered

fields in my mind, where a syllable
detonates into its own

flushed silence.
Give me a few recipes for a smidgen

of poise and a modest sense of calm.
Shall I study the absence of birds

this afternoon and the whispery
dimples of regret they leave behind?

The trees like detectives on a stake-out
hope to solve the week's

unnamed crime. We are
what we imagine ourselves

to be, but only some of the time.

Poem-Logic

What does it mean when I type *grapple*
and get *grape*? Does this mean

a fingertip-sized fruit is tucked
inside each word? Can *struggle*

dissolve into *strawberry*? I'm looking
for a logic to hold onto, for a way

to catalog the exact milky gray of clouds,
their nosebleed seats

to our pinprick of a human drama.
I search online for a photo of a blind

crustacean, get sidetracked
by texts urging me to renew my prescriptions,

my Rxs that eavesdrop on my heart and its
lonely violin solos set off by lack of sleep

and the evening headline.
Remipedes, I discover, live at the bottom

of the sea, are the only known venomous crustacean,
and swim on their backs. They would seem almost friendly

except for those fangs.

The circus-tent sadness of life purrs on—
obituaries stack up next to recipes for "comfy carbs"

and a photograph of the beloved burlesque dancer
who stepped off a city bus into traffic.

The hours slip like spilled drinks
from our hands, and we are left

mopping up the droplets
from the floor. I want to make sense

of abundance: the cornucopia of leaves
stained the color of tea

alongside hospitals turning away the sick.
Statistics blink from our phones—their lit screens

like panicked movie sets with
overworked crews and revised scripts.

How to balance the sanity of fear
against the bougainvillea bushes

that blush and blush throughout October?

Ghazal with Birds and Breath

". . . just the body
sparingly lit
by its uncertain promise"
—INGER CHRISTENSEN

These hands—fiddles of flesh tumbling over
the ledge of this spring day. This moment packed with small birds

and noon light sidling up my legs as if I'd signed a lifetime
contract with it. Today, I count my breath in the *bird-not-bird*

of each passing second, a whimsical but consistent abacus. I'm learning
to name things more diligently, that there is no small crevice

between *wince* and *flinch,* that *safe* can be a small bird
whose throb of throat drowns fear momentarily from a humid world.

I'm learning to be less deceived by the shapes of things. The male cardinal
is blood vessel red. Yesterday evening, one mate chirped for the other

so persistently it reduced the hour to the *Where are you? Where are you?*
of two lonely birds. The breath, flimsy lasso tethering us to each second,

soundbite of oxygen and despair; exhale of beer, cilantro, morning coffee.
Breath, do you know how ghostly you are? By *ghostly,* I mean *almost not here.*

I mean small birds have been breathing much longer than we have. I mean
my veins are a tenuous garden. I suspect this is why the monotony of small birds

comforts me as they dot the azaleas, live oaks and crumpled fences.
We are more certain of ourselves than we should be. Plots unfold around us

and we barely notice. A mockingbird's spotted, thumb-sized eggs
are being snatched by a squirrel as I type these words. I've heard a crow

can remember a human's face for three years. A body is a trembling;
a fragile nest of cells, snapshots of family reunions, the powder blue

of my mother's hydrangeas. To keep going, I follow the delicate equation
a small bird is. Van de Kamp, what will you do with your name's

allotment of land, its scattered birds and breath? These hands?

Sky Logic

Vermeer made his skies bleed
through 17th-century windowpanes—

a second-hand light, a tawny eye
pooled in a girl's quiet lap—

something he dared not depict
head on. And how to hold

even a teacup of it in one hand?
How to define this luminous seepage

across your fingers? I've seen a sky
dip its clouds

so low into a backyard
I thought I was drowning in whatever

I'd not yet done with my life.

Elegy to My Uterus with a Glass of Pinot Noir

When they told me you had to go,
I envisioned myself on a train in a 1950s
European war film, staring out
at a country I'd never see again:
its sulking borders, its brooding trees
set against the pale magentas
of an irretrievable evening.

Thick thud of an organ; swollen
thumbprint pressed against
colon, bladder, and the dangling
geography of the abdomen. I'd
never used you as other
women had, and now, before
I could claim you
as something I'd loved,
I was mourning you
like any female lead,
who knows her luck is down,
her escape plans
dwindling.

A romance without
an ounce of pinot noir poured,
without the department store colognes
of a first kiss. That's what you were to me.
A story plotless, a failed poem,
a smeared love letter,
tucked into a faulty forgotten drawer.
You dwelled, uneasy,
in my pleated darkness,
and were so hard to see—

your scars translucent, a shush
of secrets on any ultrasound film, the x-rays
blurred rain on a windowsill.

But when they snipped
the ligaments, preserving the almond eye
of one ovary, when they sliced
that slow smile across my pelvis,
(the anesthesiologist like a bartender,
his perfectly timed margarita
easing down my veins), I was lightened,
untethered. You were, after all,
the dense, straining plum, the widened,
sad-eyed fig I'd held onto
for too long—waiting,
in all your nodding patience,
for me to let go.

Plot

If I hadn't needed surgery, one ovary
misfiring and fatigued, like a bored orchid

dropping nauseous petals into the abdomen's dark.
If the body were not a jabbering house

shut to the light. If I hadn't been born
a twin, constantly divisible by two—my heartbeat smothered

by my brother so no stethoscope could find me
or predict my cat-out-of-the-hat surprise

on the day of my birth. If politics seemed less
like day-old toast reheated each dawn.

If panic didn't swell in me, like a cloud
of bobbing bees. If Madrid had not been the city

in which I learned to breathe.
What if it had been Istanbul or San Francisco?

By *breathe* I mean a certain settling into
the meandering crevices and alveoli

of the lungs, a deeper dreaming
inside myself. If I didn't adore

a cup of coffee singeing my lips
each morning, or the smudged people

in daguerreotypes. If people's remarks
didn't click and clack like shiny marbles

inside my brain, and the squirrel
didn't rotate a black acorn

manically in its glossy paws.

So This is How It Is

This week the most decisive
thing I've seen is a grackle—its neck

compressed into the blue oils
of black feathers before it kicked off

a street's curb. Lately, bodies
swerve all around me:

pebble-colored birds quiver
at the neighbor's red feeder, the shape and size

of a small doll house. Why do we insist
on offering animals little human houses?

The sun is unemployed and spits
tobacco diamonds into my backyard,

and last weekend grasshoppers
littered the sides of a highway, dry

cigarette butts flicked from someone's
1970s getaway car. I want the rain

to shake my coffee-fumed hands
and tell me everything's

going to be okay. No rain comes.
I want to stop placing the opened jar

of orange marmalade into the cupboard
with the sea salt and olive oil. I want

to stop mislabeling moments of myself.
How many times have I walked by

a violet-singed bush and not
known its name? How many times

have I woken from a dream taking place
in a city I've not been in for years? I'm sick

of missing London elevators and the green,
see-through waters of some beach

I once visited. I'm tired of rummaging around
the rooms in a French film, nudging against

a story someone else has written.
There are days the here-and-now

seems nothing more than an uneasy,
flabbergasted arrangement

of half-seen furniture, shifting
temperatures, and garbage smells

wafting over watery cocktails. Days
when the damp braille of newly-

awakened grass isn't enough
to rouse us toward a passion

for the lives we find ourselves living.
At least ice cubes never apologize

for what they are and can maintain
a certain persistent stance for hours.

I'm all for persistence and hours,
and for the glaring pink batteries

some clouds are as they putter through
June skies.

The Freedom of Lightning

I've watched lightning dangle
its bright dinner fork over my life—
a swaggering hunger to that
incandescence. How easily
the night became a dinner table
for a multitude of appetites
and my life felt suddenly
so ready to be sliced into.

As far as I know, no one's arms
have ever hugged a lightning bolt's
disco jolt, its swerving,
jagged glint. The carefree, drunken
author each bolt is. Steeple, tree, jogger
all possible characters
in the nano-second plot. To write
so recklessly with no fear of consequence!

Oh, to be a manic comedy,
all Katharine Hepburnesque,
with a roving punch line,
radiating heat five times
hotter than the surface
of the sun, to be
unapologetic, luminous.

My knees cough and whisper,
a cartilage-to-cartilage conversation.
Lightning is free of flesh's
intricate pulleys and levers. The body
a kind of sighing abacus
counting its grievances.

A Poem About the Body

Sometimes I think of the intricacy
of what resides in me—all the canals

and nicked windowsills, all the dull-lustered,
smooth-muscled

engine rooms. And the captions running
along the bottom of each scene, as if

they could begin to explain what a body is.
There's no preposition ample enough

to explain this daily, sun-breaking-out-
all-along-my-skin relationship. This rain-humming-

against-my-neck-and-ankles-as-I-cross-
the-street. This waking up to see if your

breathing body lies silhouetted
next to me. The head is an unapologetic

casket, accepting its hand-picked
chrysanthemums and flesh wounds

of regret, its dented signposts
and ragged roadkill. The head's a running

faucet shooting off into all kinds
of dubious directions.

My neighbor leaves her garage apartment
for the umpteenth time. She wears a lavender

sweatshirt, and she/her body
make their way down the driveway, through

another day of light-rinsed sparrows, dentist offices,
and the multicolored, flinching muscle

of traffic patterns. How many times have I not
considered the fact of my body

as I glossed over insect-thin print, as I
swallowed a beer's sluggish grin? Last night,

my body and I slept through another dream
of half-finished plots and women younger than me

lifting themselves demurely out of swimming pools.
I tried not to picture my life as a repeating carousel,

spinning its one allotment of swaying ponies.
Sometimes I think my body is willing to swallow

any kind of singing, even the bullet-sized bees.

After

After pausing between driveway and front door to hear a bird's rising trellis
    of pale questions
After walking by a jasmine bush with its broken fists of sad beauty
After thinking *profiteroles* for no apparent reason,
      I witness the afternoon shift from one light-rinsed foot to the next.

After crying just long enough for small stones to roll down my cheek
After remembering Madrid, the shattered teeth of its cobblestone streets,
After reading the headlines again, with their too-soon dead and fast-food
    restaurants,
      I tally words like "forgive" and "regret," weigh them on one spoon.

After rough tongues of the wind lick me into evening
After sipping a too-small margarita splitting its salty, sardonic sides
After thunder clotting the charcoal sky with gusting threats,
      I return to the warm cinnamon of your hands.

After losing my train of thought for the millionth time
After doing my taxes while doves coo and shiver in the trees
After car wrecks in another state and inflamed gums and the flickering
    marquees of another sleepless night,
      I ponder words like *exoskeleton* and the impossible tenderness of skin.

Daily Survival Guide—Take #1

Read a stanza of poetry upon waking—one with humid weather in it
and a cast of bees.

Drink one cup of green tea by noon and watch the bright,
balled-up leaves in the boiled water unfurl and float,
like mini Esther Williams doing the backstroke.

Look up from the computer long enough
to notice squirrels having sex in the backyard—
a tight tangle of tea-colored bodies, a ricocheting somersault,
with live oak as backdrop.

Be grateful for stray cats as they step precisely
through the yard's dry, uneven grass.

Shrug yourself off at regular intervals, like when
you drive past the brick funeral home
and spot police motorcycles all lined up—
a crop of sun-flecked midday metal—
and remember, a heat prickling
through your veins, the young firefighter.

Look up words like *refulgent*—a word with the textures
of heavy, floor-length curtains—and find it means
shining brightly, radiant. Roll that radiance slowly
in your mouth like a fig about to break open its tiny sun.

Read another poem at dusk—one with prickly pears
and the Texas border patrol.

Digest the news in controlled portions, like eating tiny spoonfuls
of cumin-spiced, ice-cold gelato.

Count your heartbeats in the evening—your own
private rainfall inside you.

Before sleep, settle into the first ten pages
of a Latin American novel, in which a whole paragraph
depicts the city's cobblestone streets,
their slick and uneven textures.

Self-Portrait as the Ballet Dancer
I Wanted to Be at Ten

I wanted to be a ballet dancer when I was ten—
all muscle twitch and lithe limb, all hair tied
into a disciplined knot at the top
of my head. But my body was more
tomboy then weeping willow, and
I soon learned my limbs could not weep
elegance nearly enough.

I've been reassembling myself
ever since: puzzling out the stars at night—
a silent movie with endless
closing credits—or a possum I recently drove by,
its chest a soft walnut cracked open
in the middle of the city street.

I like to tally what is around me,
store it in a book of fingerprint-
dusted questions tucked under
my arm, the one with freckles
trickling down it in the pattern
of a drowsy parakeet.

I've learned how my body works
over the years—at night, my torso
sleeps in the shape of a tear.
Don't feed me broccoli or I won't
be able to account
for the aftermath.
I have arthritis creeping
like a mini ice age through
the left knee, and my heart

types out a Morse code all its own
on days when the world overwhelms
with statistics, badly-parked cars,
and the curdled brow of someone's opinion.

May the weather outside my door tomorrow
offer envelopes of new air. May I rejoice
in opening them.

I've Seen White Hydrangeas as Large as a Human Head

At his bidding, Chagall turned people
and embraces upside-down. His night stars
could appear almost anywhere—blossoming
in floorboards or chairs.
If I could create a night sky equal to his:
an infinity of purple sequins, the vivid hunger
of the stars (there, I said it again, *stars*), I think
I would die content, or do I lie? Do stars know
anything of fatigue, do they subsist on more
than their aloof science and package tours
of the universe?

The neighbor's black-and-white cat
doesn't trouble himself with such questions.
He knows when to collapse
into his paws and succumb to being
a mere speck of the universe: a mini-furred
ottoman lying on a porch in July.

I've seen white hydrangeas
as large as a human head, a drugged wig
bobbing on a slender twig: a thought
larger than I'll ever guess escaped
when I held one in my hands.
The day is steadfast, keeps trying
to let me in: white butterfly like a lazy door key
opening and closing something
in the air.

I'll never hold a firefly cage
in my hands, one carved by a courtesan

in another century in Japan. What delicate
screens those cages were fashioned with,
what intricate claws to keep
the light trapped.
I've been crying more lately—spasms
rising and falling in my chest.
I see this as a kind
of private progress, as if I had grown
a new sky inside, one more
patient, less judging; one more willing
to carry an uneasy light.

Personal Glossary

I am the surprise twin, the one
who came out second, who breathed
the dustless air of the incubator—
cushioned in its mollusk grip for a month
(see: *controlled environmental
conditions*).

Sweetie Pie my mother called me
because, supposedly, I was not
sweet enough.

I am the *worrywart* after school
who paced the kitchen linoleum floor.
My hours alone in the house
with its winter breath. Each window
a wan glint; a warm mug of *Lipton Tea
(established 1893)* in my hands—
my milky mirror, my food sibling.

I am a name tangling
in another's mouth: *Alex*, *Big Al*
(because of my broad shoulders),
Alexander (I was mistaken for a boy
when playing with my brother). What about
the fog-throated waltz of a name
I wanted to call myself?

I'm 28 and in Madrid with its ammonia-rinsed
café floors, its dry, pointed leaves
scuttling across pavement,
the muddy-smeared Goyas hanging
in a nearby museum. In December,

I snack on *clementinas* (a.k.a. *Moroccan*
Clementines, accidental hybridization)
while waiting to teach English
to bankers, telecommunication
engineers, bone-marrow specialists.
The seedless plucked globe secure
in my hand as I peel back the acrid skin.

I am the uneasy whiff of loss
accruing inside me: my *Oma*'s mocha cake
served on scalloped plates, my father's
sly dimple and movie-star face
(look up: *1940s, William Warren*).

I am not a sky diver, an astronaut
aiming to dangle like a forlorn fig
in the firmament. I am not
a broccoli lover of any sort (see:
food poisoning; Baltimore
Chinese restaurant; 1980s).

And if I could, I would rewire
my short-circuited, panicky heart,
(try: *AFib, bad luck*) so it pulsed
with the ease of a Montreal
summer stroll, with its outdoor
big band jazz and bowls of *café au lait*,
its lavish lawns we found tucked away
in the city park.

Preferences

—*after Wislawa Szymborska*

I prefer internal rhyme, the mass humming
of a few *a's* and *o's*, the not-so-shy back-up singers

packed inside words.

Petit pois to the fatter peas
that pucker and pout like my fingers

after a too-long bath.

French toast.

I prefer sunlight splashing sporadically onto my life—
sleepy handprints of it on a book or desk, a sepia-toned

teardrop leaking down my thigh.

I prefer the body didn't have such a long memory.

I prefer black and white films, the sullen gleam
of Hedy Lamarr's coat, elaborate embroidery scrolling

down her shoulders as she's framed
for an ex-lover's murder.

Tea after 3 PM, and let it be the fingerbowl delicacy
of Darjeeling.

Mayonnaise on almost anything.

I prefer getting lost in the details.

Autumn temperatures settling in the 50s
and the huge blush of dying leaves.

Armoire to *closet*.

I prefer my husband not sobbing—his body a sail
wobbling in the winds of his grief.

When possible, I prefer spiral staircases
and back roads.

I prefer dark chocolate, its unapologetic nocturnal choices,
and not getting a call from the radiologist.

The imagination, despite its statistics
and low-flying drones.

I prefer the carefully considered sentence to the fast-paced
paragraph.

Given the chance, each sentence is a café in a train station,
where you can linger with a cup of coffee and cheese sandwich.

Broken Homage

—for J'laine

These mornings, the train whines
at the borders of this city,
nudging and insisting, and I step,
once again, into the unsteady
open palm of my yellow kitchen.
But I didn't expect this: the news
of a friend falling and hitting her head,
almost carelessly, in her garage
or basement (the torn shards
of the story already conflicting
and scattering, helpless, among us
who are living). I think of that head—
its delicate skull fat with a glossy
moss of black hair, and how I once
loved to watch her smoke a cigarette.
She slowed time down, unlatched
a foggy window in the air, with each
distracted exhale.

I try to think of that head again
as a bowl full of wet blue orchids,
or over-ripe pears, and the damp
gardens of an Eastern European city
she once lived in—the old ladies
muttering on their benches. You see,
I begin my homage and then it falters
and stumbles under my efforts.
All I have is the stone birdbath

in my apartment's backyard—its dry mouth
opened to the sky, and my sad,
asking hands wanting to hold so much
and getting instead the weightless
bouquet of my ongoing breath.

Wind Letter

You, dear one, fiddlesticks of breath
and pollen, the not-so-tremulous
correspondence of trees (if one more
catkin plunks into my coffee), you slip

your mind over my backyard-body,
then recede thinly away
into the shiver of May trees.

A day is a heist for you, a series
of surfaces: hinges on buildings,
a four-year-old girl's bangs, the underside
of azaleas, wrists, and tulips, the *of*'s, *of*'s
and *of*'s of this tiramisu world—equal parts
mascarpone and nightmare.

Are you more a crowd-of-fears panting
at my knee or a gasp-of-sweet-nothings
flirting with my ear; more friend or

fiend? Restless ripple, fidgety
feather duster, absentminded bulldozer,
today you are a pink-winged
hummingbird hovering inches
above my life but never

landing, you are the companion
whose terms I do not decide, whose
compulsions leave us behind; we are
a part of your itinerary; you are not

a part of ours. *Itinerary*—what
a whistling word—it carries its own
distances inside, its own unpacked
suitcases and trampled dandelions, its litany
of hungry roads.

June Poem

Some facts don't hesitate about
what they are, such as the *j* in *just because*

or the swamp smell of roses a day too long
in the vase. I read this morning

about the Bar-tailed Godwit, how it flies
for nine days without pausing for food,

water or sleep when migrating in early
autumn or spring. That is a patience

I've rarely known, to leap and not look down
until the task at hand is done.

And time is always there, a gray bird
with glossy eyes, alighting at the café table

next to ours, teetering alongside
our breakfast and hungry for whatever

we can give it. My eggs hollandaise,
for example, and its delicate take

on mortality—how this brunch is a meal
I will never relive in quite the same way.

Then there are the snow-dusted mountains
in a Turkish film—the protagonist

wrapped in a blanket in a rural hotel, gorgeous
curls of snow backdropping his despair.

Or the firefly I found in my study
while on a residency. It was a scrawny,

scrap of a thing, until
it lit up and grew bold in my hands.

This June has trundled along,
with an obedience I can almost admire.

It's been ripe with humidity hanging
damp lace in the trees, mosquitos biting

my ankles the minute I step outside,
and a trip to the East Coast to see my parents.

My mother moving with a new slowness
and suspicion of sidewalks and stairways,

the very ground her life has been placed upon,
but still able to don a sleeveless,

green cocktail dress and chat her way
through a Thursday night reception.

Oh, did I forget the wild turkeys
that were in the hay fields surrounding

her home? Large and dark-feathered,
high-stepping through the tall grass—

their necks jutting up here then there.

Complaint

My husband tells me of a recall
in local ice cream, how strains of bacteria
grew at a factory and hospital patients
died from drinking milkshakes tainted
with the rare *Listeria*. A name which only
makes me think of *wisteria*, and that word's
unapologetic, drag queen perfumes,
its propensity for medieval stone walls,
and what a different story
this would have made had two consonants
simply been interchanged.

I want more than this March rain, more than
the wafer-thin guarantee that is a day. I want a script
lavish with Old French verbs and the salty,
slow-opening fists of New England August waters.
I want an escape scene with an Eastern
European train and time to zoom in on
the delicate teacup clasped in the hero's
well-manicured hands before the soldiers come
and the borders change. The rain ignores
my complaint, thickens the yard's
green bushes. Its shifting pulleys and cords
a performance I'll never get to the bottom of,
as it plurals across the roads and sky, as it
opens its incessant, Hollywood eyes.

Tallulah Bankhead

—*an homage to Hitchcock's* Lifeboat

I want to almost die like this: a World War
rummaging around me—the dank swells of it,
the ink-blot clouds and rusty missteps of it.
A mink is armor, a weather system
she hangs about her shoulders. The luxury liner
buckled and gulped its way
to the bottom of the ocean. What do we save
in the aftermath of ourselves when floors
crumple, windows shatter, and our typewriter
slips like a tipsy guest over the side of the wooden
lifeboat?

Her cigarette becomes a sentence loosened
from its glittering declarations; becomes their chances
sagging forlornly in her mouth.
The ocean ominously shuffles its dark mirrors
about them. The mind a soliloquy that repeats
the same lines to no one in particular. Will she get out of this
story alive? Will her newsroom wit rebound? The plot
is omnivorous and holds no affection for anyone. And the man
they've just fished out of the water—friend or enemy?—
is dripping all over the floorboards.

This is Not a Fever

with its lava lamps of perspiration, its
blackening April skies.

This is not my husband's dream
where he moves in with friends, bumps into
a female acquaintance
as an odorless contagion
circles the neighborhood.

This is not a contagion
   of unwritten poems
   of trees
   of words like *mask* and *expertise*
   of thwarted murder plots
   of negligees of doubt

This is not a hand—tender collection of five
digits—eager beast we carry at the ends
of our arms; how we try and try.

I would rather not morph into
a statistic, by the way, with its
specific yet vague reckoning, its
daily finger-tap of grief
or hope; its relentless messaging.

But I am this poem with a metronome
tucked deep inside—an invisible
tick-tock as the day
stacks the fog, like shredded data
into the wet
green of the trees.

This is not a Caribbean island—its
rum daiquiris and sand-covered

eyelashes, its button-sized
jelly fish seeping through
the blue of my swimming suit.

This is not their stings rising out of my skin—
tender necklace
I carried on my reddened chest.

This is not an 8 AM headline
with sniffling *the's* and not-

fully-tested drugs, its *these*
and *those* sidling past

the dead bodies.
The clouds

have frayed cuffs, the street
is a waiting mouth, the

crime rate goes up or down
in direct proportion

to the number of people
gathering together.

Pollen falls, powders our cars; children
tangle in their own voices.

The Magician Speaks

I can't remember when objects
began to titter about me—

the coffee cup across the room shivered
in its white sleeve, the spoons

slid like crocodiles in the night
of their drawer.

Is to wake to the dusty blue
of white curtains, the ceiling fan's

tiny circus of blades
a sleight of hand

the body performs?

They say my long fingers can shatter
any expectation, my twitch of the wrist

drive the blade home, so a woman's
body flinches, yet keeps

its breath trapped like
a white bell inside the throat.

I say don't be distracted
by the obvious.

How long have you stared into a mirror's
endless door, its watery doubling

of your bedspread and lampshades?
This is the only way you've ever

studied your face—a reflection's
trick of light, its clumsy

philandering. We *are*
mystery.

The heartbeat is a bracelet
of holes.

There will be Some
Grand Marnier in this Poem

Yesterday was all bruise-throated clouds,
a low-lying density to everything. Even the grass
sighed its way through the day
as busses huffed and puffed,
and a violet-tinged grief seeped
into my elbows.

Now, after all the rain last night—
the lightning a panic attack of brightness,
the rain a wet body, slamming
its inconsolable weight against the windows—
I wake to air's new breath and leaves,
stacked in intricate damp piles,
like some kind of spontaneous
over-night art installation.

Other than leaves and rain, there is
some Grand Marnier in this poem.
It can be found in the letter I wrote earlier
this morning to an uncle in Holland, who
had just lost his wife/my aunt. I tried
to offer up small memories of her
on light-blue stationary. I recounted
my first sip of Grand Marnier in their living room
over twenty years ago. The thick, gorgeous,
slow-syrup of it, the sluggish ambers
of its hot glow as it wept down
my orange throat. And the realization that one sip
of a substance is sometimes enough
to notch you towards the person
you will become, to etch

the beginnings of a topography
inside you. But why does this
first come to mind when I think of my Aunt?
Why not her hands as they offered me
this drink in the tiniest of glasses?
Or her thick brown hair,
which was singeing toward gray
even back then?

And what of the leaves this morning?
Mounds of tarnished rosary beads
all tangled up in my driveway—muted,
muddy prayers no one will ever say—bundled
up in tarps and trucked off by the landlord's
lawn service. I miss them, those leaves,
even though they were bound
to be a nuisance, following me into the house
with their slender, slug-like paths
of debris, smudging their own
story across my floors, but they
were so thick and satisfied, somehow,
with their loss of the trees, so willing
and able to fall, without warning,
to the street.

Storms

Last night—the terrible cracking blues of that storm, its precise
axes of light, landed hard on the sky's shoulders. A storm
does not apologize for its decibels of delight—
its delight in drowning us in its sopping syllables
slapping the helpless windows.
We have no control when the storms decide to break
their staggering secrets over us—pummeling our frail fences
and pale ears. The body in the bed such a small snail, curled endlessly
in on itself—looking for answers that are not there
or that recede like the precise residue of a dream
moments after we've shaken ourselves free of its airports
and swerving corridors, of looking for a missing coat and laptop—
what we always thought we would have suddenly lost to us.

The storms are dumbfounded at our frank houses and two-bedroom
apartments, bewildered by the body's soft neon of skin, the lawn's
sparse and flickering grasses; the loud guttural swirl of mud in the street.
They dare us to new thresholds, each time coaxing us
to bear something so much larger than ourselves, to grow overwhelmed
less easily. I've seen how they can lower a sky until my arms and legs
are hammered in a bitter light, until all I can do is pray
for such devastating beauty to pass me by.

A Thursday Morning List of My Fears

That I won't finish this poem,
which could be envisioned
as a field of snow—all dawn-quiet
and dimpled with lavender-blues—
but is, in fact, an emptiness
I can't get used to.

That the weight I sometimes
wake up to, huddled against me
like a sleep-deprived sweater,
will ask me
its one indissoluble question

all day long, as I drink my coffee (cooling
to a rain-puddle sheen), as I stare

out the window, amazed another day
has formed itself
around me—the humid leaves

puzzling the trees, the doves
muttering among branches
like stagehands I can't see.

I want to dangle into this poem the coin-flash
of kumquats, or blood oranges imported
from Seville (I remember a blond boy,
a blue-tiled hostel, and a pitcher
of ruby-smeared, pulpy juice). And here's

another fear: the now-you see-it-
now-you-don't of memory, the slippery teases
of the mind and body, like the middle-aged
ventriloquist whose voice is second-hand—expressed

through a body he's groomed
with his own hands, a body whose terms
he assumes he understands.

And what are the terms? That the universe sags
indifferently with the minor ruptures
of sidewalks and surgeries, that my life
will steadily gather its list of ongoing *itises*—
gastritis, esophagitis—
and my heart's uneven percussiveness,

which plays like a bandmember
reading from the wrong score
and enjoying it?

Or that I won't figure it out fast enough, how to
love you best, how to rumple your hair,

how to notch my body against yours
to fend off time's tiny, omnivorous
hammering, and how to prepare a strawberry

shortcake that will blow your whole childhood
through your mouth as you swallow it.

Shadow and Tail

Wildflowers bleed yellow and scarlet along the interstate,
the sky opens its staring eyes. All is good
until the squirrel jumps out across the road,
and we feel that body's soft fist
under one wheel. Then the next. A decidedly
compact and visceral death.

Next day, squirrels in our backyard grasp the trees.
A furred syntax moving along the swerve
of oak branches and city wires, a splayed-foot
Barnum & Bailey act. Their genus, *Sciurus*, derived from
the Greek for *shadow* and *tail* because they reside
under the shade of their sumptuous tails. Now a squirrel
equals for me its umbrella of portable darkness. I am juxtaposed

against more than I can keep count of: garden hoses like sleeping
snakes on the pebbled ground, the landlord's dusty trellis
with one shrunken rose, an unsolved murder/suicide that takes place
three blocks away and I hear of only days after it happens,
and the rhododendron leaves on a nearby bush, fat and shining
as elegant serving spoons.

How to Write a Short Poem

I'll leave out the buzzards I just saw—
black specks slow-circling above

the bright trees, their hunger
denting the sky. I won't include

you, my love, splattering enchilada
sauce all over your linen shirt

the other night. I'll avoid multi-
syllabic words like *recidivism*

or the *hippopotamus*—its ability to devour
70 lbs. of grass in one day. I'll remove

people pointing fingers at other people,
percentages of the sick on the rise.

I'll leave in, for now, the *Pandora* ad
pushing a new product for women's UTIs,

and the cloak-and-dagger role algorithms play
in deciding our desires. The red-striped peppermints

in baskets at every restaurant in my childhood
might not make it, and the breeze

that cupped my hair in its invisible hands
a few hours ago, like the small child I will never have,

has a 50% chance of staying in.

Worry Poem

—*after Barbara Ras*

I worry about the sighing
of my mother's bones

each time we hug.

That a tornado-sky, that low-
humming, humid clutch of clouds,

will zero in on my heart one June night.

I worry that I won't hide under the butcher-block
table nearly fast enough

to dodge the bullets, sooty rain,
golf-ball-sized hail, and pigeon shit

a life can happily fling our way.
I worry I'm just a story

tucked inside other stories,
like the hatboxes

my grandmother stored in her dank,
Rhode Island basement.

A teetering stack
with department store names

like *Bonwit Teller* printed in black
dusty script across the round lids.

And let's not forget the invisible:
the mosquito the size of a torn

eyelash, the grudge that lodges
in your chest for years, and the virus

mutating with the giddiness
of a party guest who keeps

pouring herself new cocktails
from the vodkas, gins, and tequilas

lined up at the bar
by some generous host. I worry

I worry too much.
I am not the problem solver

our world craves. I am no beekeeper,
no geneticist mapping DNA.

I'm a shy activist and a distracted
cook, inclined to burn boiling milk

and peas, to leave the tea kettle
shrieking. Each thought

a firefly with its tipsy glow
careening inside my head

as if it could answer a question
I've not learned to ask yet.

Thunder: Take #132

Backstage they hammer
with perfectly-weighted gavels

sheets of bruised metal
that boomerang about your

ears. An audience gathers
in the sky. They applaud

with damp fingers; they jangle
their sepia-toned baubles.

If a cloud were a guitar,
it would plump with sadness

and then weep out
in increments

its pent-up, glossy sentiments. If a cloud
were a middle-aged *obrero*

from Madrid, it would spit casually
into back streets

its olive pits and
butts of cigarettes. A cloud

can wear stiletto heels
and ground those ashen,

grainy tips into your
unsuspecting,

dream-stuffed ears. Weather can hoard
pitted gravel in your mouth,

pool iris-shadows in the inner-
cup of an elbow. Eerie with foreshadow,

this summer afternoon tips
toward the barroom fatigue

of *film noir*. The windows
so dense with an after-hours

shot of *crème de menthe*
you're sure your life has taken on

the professional dusk of a shutter-
closing fade out.

You Know It's Been a Long Day

Each week is a marionette
pulled by time's ungainly strings,

so I'll breakfast on verbs today:
resuscitate, smolder, gaze. Hungers

hunker inside of me:
the unwritten poem, the trip

to the Caribbean that didn't take
because of a passport decidedly

out-of-date. Meanwhile, the harbor purrs
beyond the field. The red fox tiptoes his way

across my mother's morning porch. Snow
is footprints of snow and nothing more.

I have a theory that our plates of food
stare back at us trying not to pass judgment.

Such daily thoughts keep
the five-year-old alive in me despite

the mounting evidence that a life
can build its tragedies in mindful,

unstoppable degrees. I want my mother
to stop asking me where we parked the car

as we shop for Christmas gifts: a mermaid doll
for a niece, suspenders for my stepfather,

who keeps hitching up his pants after meals.
I don't want to care where my mother last placed

her shopping list. Instead, we can live by our wits
from one grocery store aisle to the next

and happen upon her favorite pound cake mix
as if it were as rare as a Matisse print—

astounded at our sheer luck.

Sleep: A Report

Oh, elusive lullaby of the body,
porthole into the brain's watery depths,

last night you had me fretting
over deadlines again—

deadlines, what a term
to carry with us as we wade

through our days without the soft
clutch of our beds,

a bullseye of panic
pinned to our to-do lists,

a grim nod to our buttercup-
dusted mortality.

Other nights, empty rooms
buoy up inside of me,

and I find myself organizing
a literary event, where each guest

must present a hardboiled egg to enter.
Who the featured speaker is,

is never mentioned. My dreams
decidedly weak on backstory

and event planning. Despite
the muddy fields that I half-remember

upon waking, and the snow
in a country I've not seen

for years, despite the dead
talking to me with teacups

in their hands, sleep,
you are a crawl space

my body finds each night,
and, together, we dig and dig

past gravity and the need for doors
to have hinges, into what the body carries

with or without our permission.

NOTES

"A Partial Cento with Middle Age Embedded in It" cites the following
poets and writers in the order in which their lines appear: 1–2 Veronica
Golos from "A Bell Buried Deep"/ 9–14 Dan Gunderman of *New
York Daily News*: "Teens arrested after rock thrown from overpass
kills man inside car" October 20, 2017 / 31–32 from *Inspector Lewis*
"One for Sorrow," Season 9, Episode 1 /37–39 Laura Kasischke from
"Gingerbread."

"Preferences" was inspired by Wislawa Szymborska's wonderfully
candid list poem "Possibilities" from *Nothing Twice*, 1997, translated by
S. Baranczak & C. Cavanagh.

I could not have written "Worry Poem" without first encountering
Barbara Ras's beautiful poem: "In the Last Storm I Tried to Write the
History of Secrets," included in her 2021 collection *The Blues of Heaven*.

ACKNOWLEDGMENTS

The author wishes to thank the editors of the publications in which these poems first appeared, sometimes in earlier versions:

AMP: "Broken Homage" and "Wind Letter"

ArtsAliveSA.com: "Dear Time,"

Cider Press Review: "Self-Portrait as the Ballet Dancer I Wanted to Be at Ten"

Great Weather for MEDIA: "Writing Exercise with No Birds in It" and "Ghazal with Birds and Breath"

Lake Effect: "Storms"

Nine Mile Art & Literary Magazine: "Noon" and "So This is How It Is"

Prairie Wolf Press Review: "The Sound Engineer with His Castanets and Feathered Pillows"

Sweet: A Literary Confection: "Sleep: A Report"

Switchgrass Review: "There will be Some Grand Marnier in this Poem"

The Texas Observer: "Shadow and Tail"

Tahoma Literary Review: "Elegy to My Uterus with a Glass of Pinot Noir"

Taos Journal of International Poetry and Art: "The Freedom of Lightning" and "A Poem about the Body"

The Windward Review: "A Thursday Morning List of My Fears," "Thunder: Take #132" (as "Thunder: Take #1"), and "Sky Logic"

Writing Texas: "Plot," "After" and "If I Were the Writer of My Own Spy Thriller"

"This is Not a Fever" was published in the anthology: *Contra: Texas Poets Speak Out*, published by Flowersong Press, 2020.

"The Sound Engineer with His Castanets and Feathered Pillows" was reprinted in *Hineni Magazine* (hinenimagazine.com).

I am very thankful for the fellow poets, loved ones, and friends who accompanied me on this bookmaking journey. Without their honesty, astute insights, and patience, this book would not be what it is. Thank you to the poets in the Señor Veggie poetry group who inspired me to keep writing my poems when I thought I had no time to do so: Jim LaVilla-Havelin, Natalia Treviño, Naomi Shihab Nye, Carmen Tafolla, Lisha Garcia, Ignacio Magaloni, and more! Huge hugs to my "Little Death" poets who shared thoughts on poems, literary conversation, feisty debate, and wine when it was truly needed: Jenny Browne, Sheila Black, Amie Charney, Eileen Curtright, and Laura Van Prooyen. A big shoutout to the careful readers of the earlier versions of this book, who offered pivotal suggestions: Sheila Black and Joni Wallace. Mostly, I am grateful for my husband, William Glenn, who is my *media naranja* and creative partner in life, and for Laura Van Prooyen, who is a wonderful editor and poetic guide.

ABOUT THE AUTHOR

 Alexandra van de Kamp is the Executive Director for Gemini Ink, San Antonio's Writing Arts Center. Her two earlier collections of poems are *Kiss/Hierarchy* (2016) and *The Park of Upside-Down Chairs* (2010). She has published five chapbooks, including *Dear Jean Seberg*, which won the *2010 Burnside Review* Chapbook Contest. Her poems have been published nationwide in journals such as the *Cincinnati Review, Connecticut Review*, the *Texas Observer, Denver Quarterly, Washington Square, Cider Press Review, Sweet: A Literary Confection*, and *Tahoma Literary Review*.